Brand Your
MINISTRY

Brand Your
MINISTRY

James S. McBride

Dominion Publishing
Baltimore, MD

Cooke, Phil. "The Art of Branding."
*Http://ministrytodaymag.com/outreach/marketing/16477
-the-art-of-branding.* Ministry Today, 1 Jan. 2008. Web.

Fogg, Steve, and Phil Cooke. "10 Common Branding
Mistakes That Churches Make." *www.stevefogg.com.*
N.p., 21 Nov. 2012. Web.
Unless otherwise indicated, scripture quotations are from
the Holy Bible, King James Bible, New International
Version®, NIV ®, Copyright ©

For more information about the title, please contact:

Dominion Publishing
www.gregdjohnson.net
Baltimore, MD
printgreg@yahoo.com

Book Cover designed by:
Mr. Gregory D. Johnson

Printed in the United States

ISBN-1545215634

Dedication

I give total honor to my Lord and Savior Jesus Christ who has given me the intellectual ability, time and talent to produce this book. I am eternally grateful of your unconditional love that drew me to You. My life is worth living because You live in me. I dedicate this book to my family: my grandmother Lula Johnson who has been a major support to me since birth. I am a living epistle of your prayers; my parents James McBride and Bernadine McBride-Smith who were told they couldn't have children; however, God made a way for me to enter into the world; my godchildren Brianna McIntyre and Jadon Milton whom I cover and pray for; my godparents Ron & Myrus James and Lamont & Terry Watkins; and the entire McKiney village. I also dedicate this book to my support team and spiritual family: my mentor Gregory Johnson (You have worn many hats in my life such as brother, father, friend, confidant. Your influence has made a lasting impact in my life. I'm in debt to you.), Aunt Barbara Johnson, Auntie Peggy Taylor, Aunt Charlene Fitch, Dr. Jovan Walker, Kendra & Jerald McIntyre, Breyon Preston, Jamie Haynes, Pastors Chris & Jekia Ledbetter, Elder Ke'Andre Lucas (my brother for life), Bishop Carl & Lady Shelia Montgomery & Harvest Time Covenant Fellowship (you were the first to give me a chance and I am forever grateful), Dr. Fondrea Lewis & the Greater Glory Church (your words and your overall presence blessed me when I first met you), Pastor Issac & Mother Freddie Joy and their daughter Frederica, Bishop Cuffia, Pastor Lamont & First Lady Angela White, and Aunt Sharon Greene. A special shout out to the WEAA Gospel Grace Family (Jamal McCullum, Derrick Fletcher, and Courtney Scott), my high school English teacher Mrs. Laquisha Hall for speaking greatness over my life even when I wasn't in a position to receive it, Mr. Jamal Evans for teaching me about the media industry, Dr. Kevin Daniels, Nancy & Robert Wallace, and Frederica & Levi Coates, thank you for planting various seeds of wisdom and encouragement, and especially pushing me to this place where I am today.

Contents

Introduction

"Get ready! Your ministry will never be the same after reading this book."

As a citizen of two worlds, how do we represent God in this natural world effectively? This is the question many pastors and ministry leaders often think about. As Kingdom citizens in this earthly world, we have a mandate to represent our God with Kingdom excellence. For the Bible declares we are in this world but not of this world. My earnest prayer is that Matthew 6:10 "Thy kingdom come. Thy will be done in earth, as it is in heaven." will filter its way into your ministry. This book will help you present God in an innovative and strategic way. One of my goals in the earth is to see the advancement of God's Kingdom in the world. I will often use this phase, "Your Brand is Jesus Christ." He is the foundation we build upon in the very image we represent.

We could not be carriers of the gospel if we didn't have a Savior so before you start reading the chapters remember everything we do is about Jesus Christ and the up building of His Kingdom, and our brand needs to represent that. This book is going to provide information, wisdom and guidance to those whom are looking for the "What's Next."

Chapter I

Why Your Ministry Needs Public Relations

Public Relations is the tool that helps the organization (the church) to develop, redevelop, or maintain relationships with their respective publics and stakeholders (the congregation, potential congregation members, and the community) through communication skills and tools. This structured method of communication wasn't developed until the 1920's which was made famous by pioneers Edward Bernays, Ivy Lee, Carl Bynoir, and John W. Hill.

But I believe the One who over 2,000 years ago defined public relations was Jesus Christ. He didn't have a practitioner to help guide Him on what His brand was but He acted out what was prophesized in the Book of Isaiah. He was His own brand. So my question to you is, "Are you a good representative of the brand God has created you to be?"

Jesus actually had a strategic campaign where His message and goal was to spread the Kingdom of God across the land. In public relations the situational analysis is apparent where God wrapped Himself in flesh with the core problem in mind of saving humanity. His objective was to have the believer to bear witness through His Word and actions which would prove to the world that He is Lord. His strategy and tactics were miracles, signs and wonders.

One of His tactics was that of proximity. He

wasn't afraid to be seen with those whom were the underrepresented, the ostracized, poor, sick, and afflicted. His presence not only left an indelible impact with those whom needed a change in their lives, but His love touched those whom weren't seeking a change. From the conversation He had with the woman at the well, to the man that had leprosy, to the thief that hung of the cross, He shared the truth in a way that was vastly different than the Pharisees. He was different. And the people were drawn to Him.

He created a brand that started by word of mouth. His fame was spread abroad to other regions. The countrymen couldn't stop talking about the miracles, signs and wonder this carpenter's son performed. Through His ministry, He changed behaviors and mindsets and created a culture for generations to follow.

To sum it up public relations is a very important tool for your ministry and brand. In the 21st century the world is the most knowledgeable in terms of basically everything including ministry. You can google how to create ministries and plant churches. With saying that I believe that all ministries should use public relations as one of their tools to feel the pulse of their audience, congregation, and potential ministry followers.

In the following chapters you will understand that public relations will help to differentiate your ministry from other ministries, create your own identity in ministry, and create goals and objectives that are measurable and obtainable. By using public relations, it will help you to send messages (your message should be

Jesus Christ) to your target audience. This book will simplify the key things you will need to know about public relations and how it relates to the church.

Chapter II

Be Strategic

Many church websites I have visited fail to differentiate themselves from other ministries. They use the same "cookie cutter template" that has been reused time and time again. On social media you see flyers with the same logo, the same design, and in some cases the same name for their respective ministry services. This lack of originality has even crept into the way some preachers deliver the Word on Sunday morning. Instead of standing in their uniqueness God has created them to be, they take clichés and catch phrases from prominent speakers and try to sound original. One would have to ask, "Do these leaders trust God wholly to bring out the best in their ministries?"

Ministries that are original and strategic didn't happen overnight. It took years of preparation, trial and error, opportunities, investment of time, money, energy, and tears; sacrifice and determination, to name a few. For these ministries it's not only what people see through their websites and messaging, but it's also who is behind the scenes to ensure the branding is evident. These particular ministries have a strategic communication team that works with the pastor and the executive leadership of the ministry.

The communication actions team (CAT) helps to create a difference of how the ministry is presented on all platforms, even down to the colors that are used. In other words, everything is strategic. On this team your ministry needs creative, intellectual minds. The mother of the church or the head of the deacon board may not be the best suited people for these positions. I suggest your team should consist of individuals that have taken communication courses, think critically, will do the requisite research and most importantly are Spirit led. That should be your core group, and if other individuals are willing to learn the craft and sit under your core group then you will have a well-staffed communications action team.

Ideally the team should consist of five to seven people; this will allow the work to be spread out among the teammates. As a ministry leader, you must welcome the ideas the CAT can contribute to the success to your organization. Here are some tips of how you can utilize the CAT.

Trend Analysis: A trend analysis is a

method of analysis that allows traders to predict what will happen with a stock in the future. This type of analysis will help you identify where your community at large is going and how you can fit and adopt your ministry in a changing environment. This will bring out both the community's needs and the congregation's needs for your local ministry.

Communications Audit: A communications audit is a comprehensive evaluation of an organization's ability to send, receive and share information with various audiences within the organization. This will help identify the following: Are your leaders friendly? Is the leadership reachable? Is your ministry community friendly? Is your ministry different from others? Do you meet or listen to your congregation's needs? With your social media platforms, do you respond to your messages and follower posts?

Strategic Planning: Strategic planning is an organization's process of defining its strategy, or direction, and making decisions on allocating its resources to pursue this strategy. I suggest you hire someone that plans your entire landscape of how you are going to reach your mission and vision. This is good for leadership to identify the needs of the mission and vision so they can find their niche and work the vision in their respective way. The CAT makes sure that based on the leadership, the strategic plan is fit to the leader's making.

Labor Relations: A labor relation is the relationship between the management of a company or organization and its workforce. In a church environment it creates proper communication and maintains the relationship between the executive team (Pastoral Staff) and the leadership team (Elders, Deacons, Ministers, and other Leadership heads). When the executive and leadership teams come together to discuss Kingdom business, it should be in an environment that not only permits honest dialogue but the meeting should be conducted in a fitting and orderly manner. However, sometimes when meetings take place, unfortunately the opposite occurs. When church growth becomes stagnant, the pastoral staff lashes out and blames the leadership team. Leaders undermine their team members when knowingly withholding information which leads to chaos and confusion. When emotions run high and are out of control, the pastoral staff and/or the leadership will go as far as to belittle a person's ideas or disparage a person's integrity. When an organization recognizes the importance of labor relations, it will treat all members with respect and love.

It is important that you fully utilize and rely on the expertise of the communications action team. When they have access to the church's resources (quarterly reports, newsletters, monthly productivity meetings notes, etc.), this will not only assist them to understand your vision, but it will be the catalyst in making the vision a reality to the public.

Chapter III

The Posture of a Brand Ambassador

Public Relations or Strategic Communications is an evolving entity where things can change for the better or worse, and as a brand ambassador of your local ministry or ministry brand, you have to keep an open mind and take calculated risks (walk in faith). In my time of consulting clients, they would always compare their ministries to their peers and prominent ministries. They think that they can do some of the extraordinary things that most ministries of prominence can do but they choose to find shortcuts to try to reach those heights. As a brand ambassador you need to find your own lane.

There is so much ministry out there that you can find an area that is a need and maximize that area to where you are an expert in that field. For example, if you are a spirit led ministry, create events, offer educational sessions, and build engagement with your community on how to lead a spirit filled life. In other words, create a brand around that entity. If you work in the prophetic, build a brand around the prophetic. If you are a biblical scholar, your focus should center on education in the Word of God.

When you decide what your ministry niche is, there is an excitement that can't be contained. As the song says, "Oh, the joy that floods my soul." You're no longer seeking an identity in ministry. In fact you will invest time and energy to find out EVERYTHING you can about your niche. And your communications team will work with you as they constantly survey the area on current trends and forms to keep you brand alive and relevant.

My suggestion to the pastoral leaders on being Brand Ambassadors--you need to be you and remember there is only one you. In a society that is constantly changing and people are frantically trying to keep up with the times, in times of transition, don't lose your identity. Whether reaching out to people whom feel left behind and are seeking hope or interacting with those that are content, people want to see authenticity. In this 21st century where people can google any topic and become unofficial subject matter experts, they can spot a fake and a phony without being spiritual. When you give false hopes, make promises and then break promises, and fail to follow through with your word, your brand will be tarnished and bashed both by word of mouth and on social media.

Remember that anything you do in public is up for public scrutiny. Your actions, how you talk, where you appear at social events, your political views, whom you invite to your church, even down to your viewpoints biblically can affect your brand. If they don't align with Jesus Christ, your brand will fade away and become obsolete.

Chapter IV

Measureable Goals

Topachievement.com/smart defines measurable goals as the following: "Establish concrete criteria for measuring progress toward the attainment of each goal you set. When you measure your progress, you stay on track, reach your target dates, and experience the exhilaration of achievement that spurs you on to continued effort required to reach your goal."

Public Relations (PR) is an important part of our society because it requires us to be honest and accurate as to how we use our strategies and tactics in a timely matter. PR make us evaluate our efforts while asking the question "Will our methods really work?"

In order to measure and evaluate our strategies and tactics, PR experts use the S.M.A.R.T chart which means:

SPECIFIC

MEASURABLE

ATTAINABLE

REALISTIC

TIMELY

Specific - A specific goal has a much greater chance of being accomplished than a general goal. To set a specific goal you must answer the six "W" questions:

*Who: Who is involved?

*What: What do I want to accomplish?

*Where: Identify a location.

*When: Establish a time frame.

*Which: Identify requirements and constraints.

*Why: Specific reasons, purpose or benefits of accomplishing the goal.

Measurable - Establish concrete criteria for measuring progress toward the attainment of each goal you set.

When you measure your progress, you stay on track, reach your target dates, and experience the exhilaration of achievement that spurs you on to continued effort required to reach your goal.

To determine if your goal is measurable, ask questions such as: How much?

How many?

How will I know when it is accomplished?

Attainable – When you identify goals that are most important to you, you begin to figure out ways you can make them come true. You develop the attitudes, abilities, skills, and financial capacity to reach them. You begin seeing previously overlooked opportunities to bring yourself closer to the achievement of your goals.

You can attain almost any goal you set when you plan your steps wisely and establish a time frame that allows you to carry out those steps. Goals that may have seemed far away and out of reach eventually move closer and become attainable, not because your goals shrink, but because you grow and expand to match them. When you list your goals you build your self-image. You see yourself as worthy of these goals, and develop the traits and personality that allow you to possess them.

Realistic - To be realistic, a goal must represent an objective toward which you are both willing and able to work. A goal can be both high and realistic; you are the only one that can decide just how high your goal should be. But be sure that every goal represents substantial progress.

A high goal is frequently easier to reach than a low one because a low goal exerts low motivational force. Some of the hardest jobs you ever accomplished actually seemed easy simply because they were a labor of love.

Timely – A goal should be grounded within a time frame. With no time frame tied to it there's no sense of urgency. If you want to lose ten pounds, when do you want to lose it by? "Someday" won't work. But if you anchor it within a timeframe, say "by May 1st," then you've set your unconscious mind into motion to begin working on the goal. Your goal is probably realistic if you truly believe it can be accomplished. Additional ways to know if your goal is realistic is to determine if you have accomplished anything similar in the past or ask yourself what conditions would have to exist to accomplish this goal.

T can also stand for **Tangible** – A goal is tangible when you can experience it with one of the five senses, that is, taste, touch, smell, sight or hearing.

When your goal is tangible you have a better chance of making it specific and measurable and thus attainable.

I gave all of this information regarding measurable goals because I've seen ministries set goals and then over time they fall through because they weren't measurable. For example, one pastor requested consultation for planting a ministry in Baltimore, Maryland while living in Detroit, Michigan. He told me his ministry in Detroit was lacking and the Holy Spirit wouldn't let him sleep. The ministry in Michigan had 25 members and only 15 attended weekly services at the local assembly.

If he was thinking logically he should have focused on finding new innovative ways to build the ministry in Michigan instead of trying to start another church 900 miles away. This is not measurable by any means.

In addition to measurable goals, time management is extremely important to your ministry and brand. A calendar not only keeps you, your congregation and potential members apprised of launches, events, and special church services, it minimizes double booking of events and scheduling conflicts with your leaders. In this time oriented generation people sincerely appreciate when activities are well thought out, planned and executed as scheduled.

Most of the time expectations that aren't measured normally occur when ministries host events without a proper objective and goal. Some events or special services can be seen as a money game if they don't have a proper meaning. For example, if you have ten church services outside of your typical Sunday morning services and midweek Bible Study and you haven't stated why you're having the extra services, then your idea won't be as effective as you would like it to be. When measuring your ministry ideas, goals, and objectives, you need to consider timing, resources, and the congregants' participation.

Chapter V

Your Ministry Message

Your ministry message is very important to your brand. First and foremost, your message and focal point should be Jesus Christ and Kingdom building. If your ministry message doesn't center around that then your ministry is in trouble. If your mission and vision doesn't include Jesus and Kingdom building you have no ministry message.

Some ministries don't realize that when you create a mission and vision you have to live out those two entities. If your mission says you are going to create opportunities to minister to those that have HIV/AID's then in your entire ministry existence you should have created a program or a ministry where those individuals that are dealing with that illness are being provided a service whether its spiritual guidance, physical help and counsel during this ordeal. But as the ministry leader/ brand ambassador you kept your promise by fulfilling your mission which is reaching your vision.

A mission definition for ministry purposes is the vocation or calling of a religious organization, especially a Christian one, to go out into the world and spread its faith.

Your ministry message is birthed out of your mission. But I want readers to know that your mission and vision can change over the course of time. And this comes in finding your ministry niche. You need to maximize that niche by adding it into your mission and vision. For example, if faith is your niche, your mission can address areas such as building your faith, prayer and faith, faith as a lifestyle, etc. If it's healing, you should have it in your mission and vision of how to receive and maintain healing. These types of niches convey your ministry message to your publics which will attract those that are in need of those qualities. In fact your message will speak for your brand while you're not around.

Now I have some questions that will help you with your ministry message.

1. Who is your church's target audience?

2. What is your church's message? Why should

someone in the community care?

3. What are some creative, meaningful, and/or newsworthy ideas your church can generate?

4. What are the most appropriate media options for this message?

5. How do we execute the message?

Chapter VI

Greater Brand

From previous experience, I have encounter some ministry leaders that think their ministry brand is just a flyer, colors, a logo, and a website. While some of these tactics create brand identity, I need to remind you that branding is much, much more than these strategies and tactics.

Strategic Communications specialist Phil Cooke's article in Ministry Today Magazine talked about the art of branding and he gave some tools that are important when it comes to branding. These tips will be beneficial for ministry leaders and brand ambassadors.

1. **Visibility is just as important as ability.** It's important that your brand have physical presence in the arenas that fit your ministry. If your desire your ministry brand to be on the radio, do you need to be on the gospel station and/or do you want to reach the unbeliever via a secular station? Keep in mind your actions speak louder than your words. This will help your brand to gain trust among your publics.

2. **Perception is just as important as reality.** We are in a society where publics are observing how prepared we are in ministry. If we're not careful, sometimes our ministries can create our own worlds where at times they exempt themselves from perception and our actions can say a lot if

we don't watch it. From being cocky, arrogant, and not showing humility, our publics are smart and quickly pick up on these characteristics. So we have to pay close attention when our publics point out things we do on social media or in person because we unknowingly can create negative perceptions about ourselves.

3. **Being different is everything.** God has given His people many gifts, talents, and our own uniqueness that differentiates us from one another. The delivery of a sermon isn't restricted to one type of preaching style. Ministries big and small, ministries for women, men, and children are examples of what makes a ministry different. But in the 21st century there are copycats,

impersonators and individuals who have identity issues and they don't have a problem copying someone else's ministry or sermons. Even though some people have the same ministry message and goals, God created you to be unique and it's your job to discover your ministry niche.

The information that was provided is very vital for your ministry branding. As ministry leader you have to develop an identity that is of your own creation by finding your God given identity that will make you comfortable in your skin. And when you discover who you are, you won't have to try to be somebody else.

A quote from Phil Cooke easily summarizes this

chapter:

"God has given us the Holy Spirit that leads us and guides us, and God gives us Holy Intelligence where we can think on things that have never been done before. Whitty inventions and new innovations come from the Father and all He does is download it to us in prayer, dreams, and visions through His Word. What we have to do is be in communication with God."

Chapter VI

The Pitfalls of Branding

In ministry most leaders and departments have ideas on how to brand the ministry based on the current time. Most people think they are branding themselves and creating brands that evolve around them which isn't a brand for ministry. Jesus Christ was a very selfless person; He cared about others. Better yet He sacrificed His life for us so we can be free from the consequences of sin and our lives can be abundant with Him in it. As humans, we make mistakes and sometimes we don't realize the mistake until it actually happens. Branding in some ways can create some pitfalls that can be detrimental and damaging to your brand.

In the secular realm branding is used to advance the individual who is behind the brand. Some brands can be self- absorbing and are all about the positive things the individual does to sell himself for the particular purpose and mission of the brand. But in ministry branding you have to be underneath the main brand ambassador of this Gospel which is Jesus Christ. The saying I hear often that bothers me is, "I'm trying to make His name great." Well, I'm here to tell you His name is already great, He is famous, world renown and He is the greatest name in the earth. To be honest being connected and committed to Jesus Christ will give you more clout then not being connected to Him. Again you will hear me say this, "Your Brand is Jesus Christ".

Strategic Communications specialist Phil Cooke gave some tips from his book Branding Faith which ministries need to avoid while branding their ministry. This information will enlighten your mindset when it comes to branding.

1. **Use large/successful church names in a church name**

"Don't be <u>a carbon copy of another church</u>. There are many relevant names that your church can use. Linking your name to a successful church is setting yourself up to fail. Rather ask yourself what is it that makes us distinctive? What is the story we have to tell?

On a side note, I've seen really awful names that copied a large church. Honestly, what were they thinking? That people are driving around looking for churches and thinking that's a church we must visit because it's the True Jesus Church, not like that other church that obviously is the pretend Jesus church." Phil Cooke

2. The building is the hero photo

"Want to make your brochure and website really come alive? Put your church building on it!

No. Don't. Please.

The church is about people, not a building. Visitors are not interested in your building; they are interested in your story, community, faith expression, what you stand for, why you exist, not a building." Phil Cooke

3. The Pastor is the hero photo

See previous rationale.

4. Only use trendy names

"I also see mostly generational ministries use trendy, abstract names which is fine, if you lead with the generational age group rather than the name. For example 'Are you a teenager? Come along to Vibe and connect into community on Tuesdays'. Don't do this 'Come along to Vibe and connect into community on Tuesdays' ". Phil Cooke

5. Use words that don't reflect who you really are

"Words like, contemporary, inclusive, edgy, traditional, young families, teenagers all describe a point in life or a way of expressing how you 'do' church. If you are going to summarize yourself in these ways then you need to be accurate. If you say that you are a church for young families, you better have lots of young families and not just aspire to having them." Phil Cooke

6. Only talk about your church

"Instead of websites or marketing collateral that just talk about what their own church is about, church leaders need to ask what are the meaningful ways they can be of service? Is it a life stage, or a pain point where their church can help bring healing? It's not just about what a church is about, but how a church can help." Phil Cooke

These pitfalls of branding can bring a different type of spirit on the individual that is trying to be at the forefront of the brand of the ministry. My experiences with former clients pointed out some of these pitfalls. I have encountered pastors that wanted to brand themselves for more speaking engagements, while some churches' goals wanted to reach megachurch status. Even some gospel artists wanted singing engagements at churches where they might not have a relationship with and wanted me to get them a gig (that's not even my job).

I must again emphasize that ministry branding is all about Jesus Christ. If you aren't showing any attributes of Christ in your brand then you are in trouble. The 21st century unbeliever knows an egotistical leader from a mile away.

When they visit and experience your ministry they can feel that cult like spirit that is cultivated in the atmosphere. I'm not saying that your ministry is a cult but if you look at the definition of what is a cult you will see it is all about one person and that one person isn't Jesus Christ. Leaders, Pastors and Bishops don't put yourself in front of God because first it's wrong and, second, God gets angry. And I don't think you want to make Him angry.

Chapter VIII

Target Audience

In public relations we conduct research to figure out the behaviors and mindset of the audience of the particular campaign that is being targeted. But ministry branding has to identify that audience we all are trying to reach. In the 21st century there is no general audience. We see that everything has been literally broken down from gender, age, location, and lifestyle. Then we found out that particular audiences communicate differently from other audiences. For example during the Depression Era, the public communicated by radio, newspaper, and letter writing. Today, the evolution of technology makes communication easier, faster and convenient. The baby boomers love to communicate through email, text, and even social media with Facebook being at the top as one of their favorite types of social media. Generation X and millennials also love social media. On it they find love, build relationships with other people, search for jobs, get the latest news and even watch television and view movies.

By using the entities listed below, you can pinpoint the types of strategies to use in order to reach your audience.

Geographic: region, city size, statistical data.

Demographic: gender, age, race/ethnicity, life stage, birth era, household size, marital status, income, education, occupation.

Psychographic: personality, values, lifestyle, needs.

Though a daunting task, keep in mind that the more information you gather about your target audience, the better the position you'll be in to foster relationships and meet needs.

Chapter IX

Strategies & Tactics

Now comes the fun part of public relations-- the execution of your big idea and your measured goals. When it comes to our strategies and tactics, most of us think ahead at times to the point where we forget that we need to have a good reason to produce them. Strategies and tactics consist of events, media pitching, social media campaigns, television, radio, print media, and endorsements. Here is a list of strategies and tactics that will help you to brand your ministry effectively.

- Ads in newsletters
    - including HOA newsletters and community associations

- attempt to get small ads in all local newsletters and on community websites

- Member mailing lists (e.g. letters, group emails, special invitations, newsletters, etc.)
  - frequently send mailings to the launch team members – at least once per month in addition to group emails

- Stationery with church logo and name (ongoing use)

- Adopt a local cause/charity

- New movers program
  - send welcome letter and card to new residents

- Websites
  - get website linked to as many community sites as possible

- Word of mouth
  - community networking—launch team constantly inviting friends

- Yellow pages
  - Small ad in phone book

- Sponsorships of community events and teams
  - sponsor summer/fall kids sports team

- Flyers
  - recruit launch team members
  - advertise general information and events
  - visit selected carrier routes monthly

- Giveaways (first touch)
  - to be given away at events when possible

- Brochures
  - new church brochure that can be used as first touch for visitors
  - could also be mailed to homes

- Special giveaways
  - pens and magnets, gift cards, televisions, vacations

- Direct mail letters
  - saturate local carrier routes in the area near the time special events are offered: 3-5 carrier routes per mailing
  - target selected carrier routes at least monthly

- Portable outdoor signs
  - at least four large A-frame or real-estate type signs

- Flyers
  - for car windows, handouts, store counters, store windows

- posted for each event and seminar

- Direct mail postcards
  - 4 inch card mailing x 30,000 just prior to first public services
  - mailed during the month prior to launch
  - possibly mailed at other times (if extra cards are available)

- Special newsletters
  - mailed at least once to the community located near the meeting location
  - selected carrier routes to target events

- Participation in local community and civic events
  - determine opportunities and get involved in as many as events as possible
  - rent booths, tables, etc.

- Posters
  - use on a case-by-case basis for large outreach events and grand opening

- Outdoor banners
  - at least one 4' x 10' vinyl banner with basic information - for use at outreach events and placed in front of the Sunday meeting location

- Free publicity (Public Relations)
  - press release kit
  - free listings of church events

- community interest articles released in conjunction with large events and start of worship services - ongoing with emphasis prior to launch and at large events

- Magazines (builder/community magazines)

- Video brochures (DVDs)

- Indoor banners

- Speaking Engagements (community organizations)

- Radio (underwriting , donations for advertisement)

- Television

- Billboards

- Fundraising

  - galas
  - special dinners
  - entertainment events

- **Social Media**
  - respond to every comment
  - post often
  - share stories
  - comment on current events
  - livestream the sermon

These tools will give you a jump start on your ministry branding, and you should see results come in as you execute these tactics and strategies. I suggest you do three to four tactics quarterly so you can measure your results to see what worked and what didn't work. In public relations everything might not be measurable at the time but that's when your research kicks in and you know who your target audience is. And once you identify your target audience (millennials, seniors, middle aged people, children, etc.), this will make your strategies and tactics easier to track.

Chapter X

Brand Your Ministry

Are you ready to brand your ministry? Are you ready to take your ministry to the next level? Is your mind racing to get started on your strategic communications campaign for your church? I hope the contents of this book will spark Kingdom excellence in your spirit and in your local ministries. When we do things the right way God honors our works and bestows His blessings on them. 1 Corinthians 14:40 states, "Let all things be done decently and in order." God loves order and public relations create an order for your brand.

Always remember branding requires all of your ducks to be aligned in the right places and will require time, effort and a proper budget to be successful. My prayer is that you evaluate your ministry and the brand it represents, then ask yourself, "Is my brand, my focal point Jesus Christ?" If the answer is yes then go forth in using tactics and strategies with the mindset of glorifying God. Everything we do has to represent the Kingdom of God, and your brand will help you reach people and use different platforms that our forefathers weren't able to do. In this book I showed you have to build proper public relations campaigns and our Lord and Savior was the first campaign that was ever created. And His brand sets the example we all should follow. One thing Pastor Fondrea Lewis shared with me after I taught a session on branding is "the message is the same but we have to change our methods." This sums it up --

develop your methods that keep the message (Jesus Christ) the same but use different, innovative techniques to present that message.

I am praying that your brand will be successful and your ministry will become better and greater than ever before.

Friend, now it's time to Brand Your Ministry!!!!!

www.ingramcontent.com/pod-product-compliance
Lightning Source LLC
Chambersburg PA
CBHW061218180526
45170CB00003B/1053